Pawprints in The Butter

A COLLECTION OF CATS

JOY COWLEY

and friends

MALLINSON RENDEL

For Wendy Pye with
love and gratitude

First published in 1991 by
Mallinson Rendel Publishers Ltd,
P.O. Box 9409, Wellington

© Joy Cowley and friends, 1991
Designed by Lindsay Missen Design Limited
ISBN 0-908606-75-3
Printed by Colorcraft Ltd, Hong Kong

MY CAT

He scratches like a hen
And growls like a dog.
He hisses like a snake.
He jumps like a frog.
He creeps like a lizard.
He climbs like a goat.
And he purrs like the motor
Of a fishing boat.

He mews like a gull.
He runs like a hare.
He pounces like a lion.
He eats like a bear.
He plays like a monkey.
He walks like a duck.
And he purrs like the engine
Of the milkman's truck.

ROBBER CAT

Sly old robber Fattyface
Has magnets on her paws
For opening kitchen cupboards
And refrigerator doors.

She robs a house, then vanishes.
All the owner sees
Are pawprints in the butter
And toothmarks in the cheese.

LAZY CAT

World War III could start in town
But our cat wouldn't stir.
Half the street could be burnt down
And she'd just sit and purr.

Aliens could land from outer space
And attack with savage cries.
While they screamed about the place,
Our cat would close her eyes.

Thunder could crash above her head,
Sirens sound in her ear.
Our cat would stay curled up in bed,
Pretending she couldn't hear.

But there *is* a noise which sends her
Leaping madly to her feet,
The sound of the old tin opener
On top of a can of meat.

TREE CAT

Bird in a tree,
Sleep, sleep, sleep.
Cat climbed up,
Steep, steep, steep.
Bird opened eye,
Peep, peep, peep.
Cat about to
Leap, leap, leap.
Bird flew away,
Cheep, cheep, cheep.
Cat slunk home,
Creep, creep, creep.

APRICOT CAT

The apricot cat said to the mouse,
'Mousie, I do love you!
Come with me to my beautiful house
With its table set for two.

And you will hear me sing:
Mousie dear, Mousie dear,
You're the sweetest thing.'

The mouse said 'No!' to the apricot cat.
'I will not go with you!
One place at your table is set for cat,
The other for mousie stew.

And I would hear you sing:
Mousie stew, Mousie stew.
You're the sweetest thing.'

LONG-TAIL CAT

Jake had a long long tail
Like the handle of a broom.
Jake slept beside the fire,
His tail across the room.

A kitten saw the tail
And thought it was a snake.
She pounced on it and bit it
And found the snake was Jake!

MEAN CAT

Some cats are as fat as cushions.
My cat is long and lean.
Some cats have smiling faces.
My cat's face is mean.

Some cats have names like Tiddles,
Fluff or Butter-paws,
Ginger, Snow or Sweetie.
My cat's name is Jaws.

Some cats eat chunky cat food.
Some think that milk is nice.
My cat eats dead blowflies
And chews the heads off mice.

Some cats play games with paper,
And roll across the floor.
When my cat wants some fun,
It bites the dog next door.

TALLEST CAT

The tallest cat in the world went by
With his head stuck in the air.
The smallest cat in the world called out,
'Is there anyone home up there?'
The tallest cat in the world looked down,
Saw nobody in the street
And said to himself, 'Well, I'll be blowed!
I think I've got talking feet!'

Waaka Harris

GHOST CAT

A couple of years ago,
A deaf old cat named Mack
Went for an evening walk
Along the railway track.
He didn't hear the whistle
Of the midnight train.
'Dead!' said the engine driver.
'We won't see him again.'
Me-ow!

The driver was mistaken.
The ghost of Mack came back
To haunt the midnight train
On that section of the track.
The driver said he saw him
Suddenly appear.
His coat was grey like mist.
His eyes were cold and clear.
Mee-ee-o-ow!

And sometimes lonely travellers
Bound for distant places,
Woke up after midnight
With pawmarks on their faces.
They gave a cry of terror
As a pale grey shape slid by,
And through the darkened carriages
They heard the ghostly cry.

M e e - e e - e e - e e - o ﹘ o ﹘ o ﹘ o ﹘ o w !

GARDEN CAT

Beware of the jungle of garden.
A cat is lurking there.
Between the tomatoes and rhubarb,
She's made herself a lair.

Feel pity for the garden rat
Who wanders out and sees
Unblinking eyes and needle teeth
Behind the row of peas.

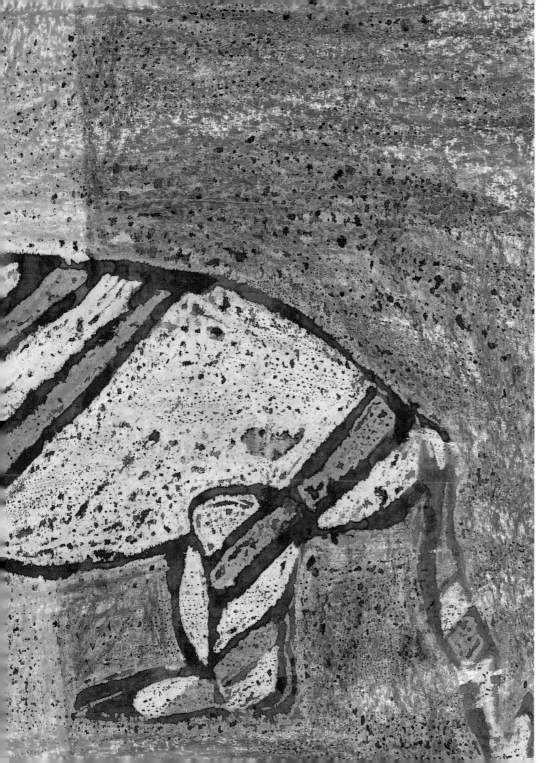

And do not think it strange
When it's time to feed the cat,
That she walks away from dinner.
Her stomach's full of rat!

GRUMPY CAT

When our black cat Fog
Waves his tail like a dog,
It's not a welcoming sight.
Dogs wag their ends
When they want to be friends.
Cats waves their tails out of spite.

When our black cat Fog
Waves his tail like a dog,
We know he is ready to fight.
We don't stay to play,
We go on our way,
Before he can scratch us and bite.

SEA CAT

There was a cat called Moggy
Who used to swim in the sea.
It made her whiskers soggy
But it got her fish for tea.

SAD CAT

Sadly, sadly, sadly,
The cat cried to the sun,
'Nobody likes me!
No, not anyone!'

Gladly, gladly, gladly,
The sun smiled at the cat.
'I like you and I love you.
Please, remember that.'

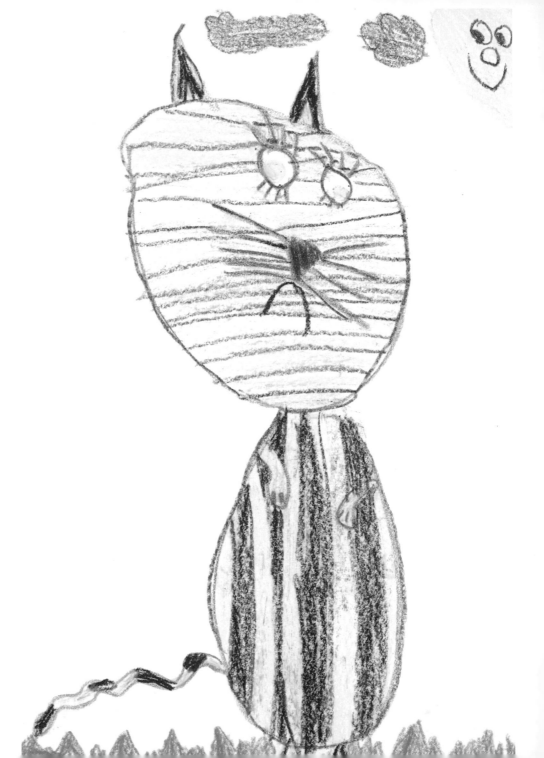

CRAZY CAT

Who stole the ball of knitting wool?
Who followed Sue and me to school?
Who fell into the swimming pool?
That crazy cat called Daisy.

Who ran around the house at night?
Who knocked down the bedroom light?
Who gave us all a great big fright?
That crazy cat called Daisy.

Who comes in with muddy feet?
Who thinks moths are good to eat?
And who's the best cat in the street?
That crazy cat called Daisy.

DANCING CAT

Smarty Girl the dancing cat
Knows where every party's at.
In fancy dress and fancy hat,
This is what she yowls-o.

'First your right paw,
Then your left paw.
One, two, three, four.
One, two, three, four.
Wriggle your tail.
Wriggle some more,
Sing and dance the meow-meow.'

She's got music in her paws.
She does a tap dance with her claws.
Her long tail sweeps the dancing floors
And this is what she yowls-o.

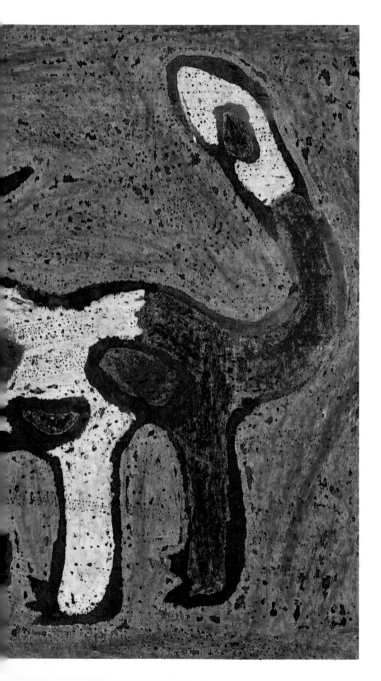

'First your right paw,
Then your left paw.
One, two, three, four.
One, two, three, four.
Wriggle your tail.
Wriggle some more,
Sing and dance the meow-meow.'

She dances home when dawn is near,
Her whiskers wet with ginger beer,
Bits of popcorn in her ear,
And this is what she yowls-o.

'First your right paw,
Then your left paw.
One, two, three, four.
One, two, three, four.
Wriggle your tail.
Wriggle some more,
Sing and dance the meow-meow.'

NEW CAT   We have a new cat Seefor.
He's big and round and fat.
Why did we call him Seefor?
It's simple. See for cat!

KITTY CAT

When Kitty cat came home from school,
Mother cat went to meet her.
She took the little kitten's bag
And gave her a hug to greet her.

'What did you do at school today?'
Mother cat fondly cried.
'I learned a foreign language,'
Little Kitty Cat replied.

Mother cat said, 'How clever!
Tell me a word of it now!'
The kitten proudly smiled at her
and said, 'Bow wow! Bow wow!'

BRAVE CAT

Mother cat goes hunting.
The kittens make a fuss.
'Do be careful, Mother.
Hunting is dangerous!'

'I'm very brave,' says Mother.
'I know how to fight.
I'll attack with tooth and claw
And you will eat tonight.'

Mother comes home from hunting
When the moon is nearly set.
The kittens run to meet her.
'Oh Mother! What did you get?'

'I've had a terrible battle,'
she laughingly replies.
'Look! I've killed six sausages
and two whole chicken pies!'

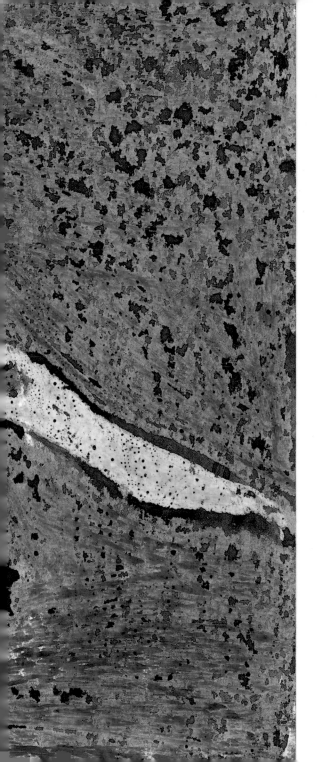

BEDTIME CAT

There's a lump on my bed,
A bump on my bed,
A furry purry hump on my bed,
And my mother said,
'Put the cat out!'

There's a growl outside,
A yowl outside,
A cold and lonely howl outside,
And my brother cried,
'Let the cat in!'

LIST OF ILLUSTRATORS

Title page	Kelvin Bigwood, Levin North School, Levin
My Cat	Charlie Tanirau, Corinna School, Porirua
Robber Cat	Lamen Pere, Camberley School, Hastings
Lazy Cat	Macaela Ward, Levin North School, Levin
Tree Cat	Tara McIntosh, Waikiwi School, Invercargill
Apricot Cat	Lauren Cairns, Levin North School, Levin
Long-Tail Cat	Lauren Juno, Levin North School, Levin
Mean Cat	Hone Reihana, Mangamuka School, Okaihau
Tallest Cat	Lachlin Beatson, Durie Hill School, Wanganui
Ghost Cat	Waaka Harris, Mangamuka School, Okaihau
Garden Cat	Logan Fui, Corinna School, Porirua
Grumpy Cat	Beth Hollinger, Fendalton School, Christchurch
Sea Cat	David Johnson, Levin North School, Levin
Sad Cat	Sarah Westcott, Durie Hill School, Wanganui
Crazy Cat	Craig Boyd, Levin North School, Levin
Dancing Cat	Moeroa Hosking, Corinna School, Porirua
New Cat	James Lloyd, Durie Hill School, Wanganui
Kitty Cat	Simone Rowe, Levin North School, Levin
Brave Cat	Marcia Gay, Hampden Street School, Nelson
Bedtime Cat	Tumu Mata, Corinna School, Porirua
Endpapers	Debbie Godsiff, Waitaria Bay School, RD2, Picton
Front cover	Moera Hosking, Corinna School, Porirua
Back cover	Jessica Chong-Nee, Levin North School, Levin

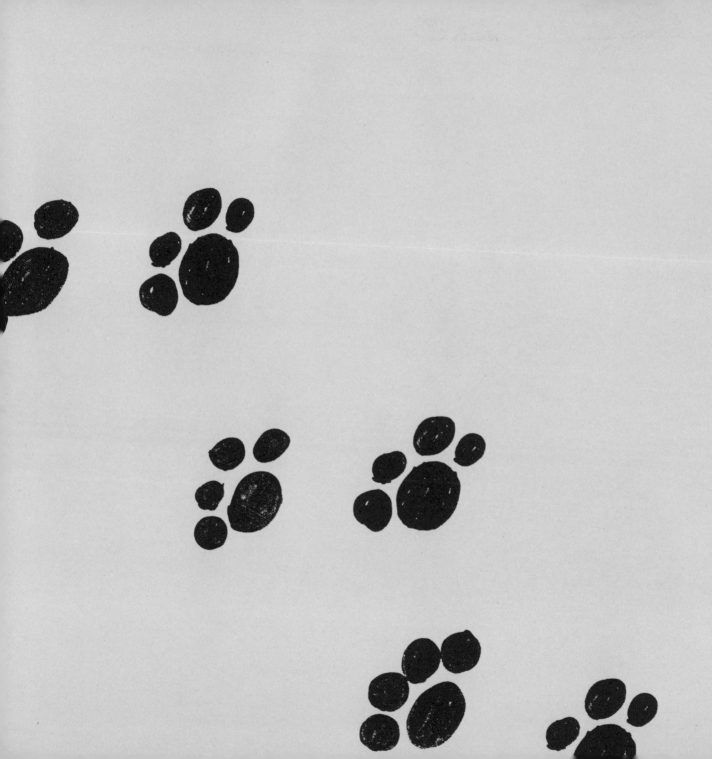